What is Hygge?

Hygge for Kids

Happy Little Viking Press

For my own happy little Vikings

Happy Little Viking Press
Christiania
København
www.happylittleviking.com

This is a little book about finding happiness in your day-to-day life.

In Denmark, this is called *hygge*.

What is Hygge?

Hygge ('hoo-gah') is a Danish word.
It is usually translated as 'coziness' or 'wellbeing' but hygge is much more than this.

Hygge is a happy way of living for adults, for children, for everyone.

Denmark is a Scandinavian country in Northern Europe that was once the home of the Vikings.

Nowadays, Denmark is known as the happiest country in the world.

Danish people are very happy.

Sometimes they feel sad or worry about things, just like everyone else.

This is normal. Life can sometimes be difficult or upsetting and Danish people know that it is OK to feel down at these times.

But Danish people have hygge every day to remind them that happiness is never far away.

So what is Hygge?

Hygge is the happiness that comes from celebrating small, simple everyday actions.

You can find hygge by curling up in a comfy chair and drinking a mug of hot chocolate, watching the rain pour down while you are safe and warm inside or sharing a bowl of popcorn with your friends as you watch a movie.

Hygge can be found almost everywhere!

Hygge is the feeling of calm that comes from opening your senses and living in the moment.

What can you hear?

What can you smell?

What can you feel?

What can you see?

What can you taste?

So why do I need hygge?

Life is busy, loud and non-stop.

This makes people stressed and anxious. Most of all it makes people sad.

Hygge helps people to stop, reconnect with the 'real' world and rediscover their own happiness.

Hygge is not noisy, stressful, expensive or complicated.

In fact, hygge is the celebration of the simple pleasures of living.

Food is an important part of hygge, as are shared moments with friends and family.

So sharing food with loved ones is very hygge!

Hygge is about making real connections with the people and the world around you, so smartphones, tablets, laptops and social media are not hygge.

How do I learn to hygge?

Hygge is a way of life in Denmark.

Winters are long and dark in Denmark and the weather is often windy and rainy.

Rather than feel sad or bored waiting for the weather to improve, Danish people find hygge in everything that they do.

You too can find hygge in your everyday life.

At first you may need to make an effort to find the hygge in your life, but soon you will get into the hygge habit!

Here are five easy steps to finding hygge in your everyday life

Use All Your Senses

The most important part of hygge is living in the moment.

This means using all of your senses to appreciate hygge – sight, smell, taste, touch and sound.

If you use all your senses to celebrate sharing a mug of hot chocolate with your friends (the way the chocolate seems to shine, the sweet smell, the rich taste, the warmth of the mug in your hand, the sound of your friends talking and drinking with you) then there is no space left for worries or sadness.

Get Comfy

Being comfy is an essential part of hygge.

You cannot be happy and uncomfortable at the same time.

So put on some comfy clothes (we even have a word in Danish for the clothes that we put on to hygge!) and find somewhere cozy to sit.

Food

Eating something delicious makes anyone feel happy, so it's no surprise that food is an important part of hygge.

Any type of food will do, it doesn't have to be fancy or expensive – a yummy cookie, your favorite pastry, a burrito or a fresh pizza.

As long as it tastes good!

Taking the time to make the food is also very hygge, like baking a delicious chocolate cake.

Friends and Family

Being with friends and family makes us happy, so it's always best to hygge with your loved ones.

Get in Touch with Nature

The natural world is very hygge – it is beautiful, calming and simple and reaches all your senses.

Danish people love to spend time outdoors and find lots of ways to celebrate nature when they're indoors too – flowers, plants or a collection of rocks or shells, they all help to make your home feel hygge.

Here is a little space for you to jot down your own hygge habits (no smartphone or social media allowed!).

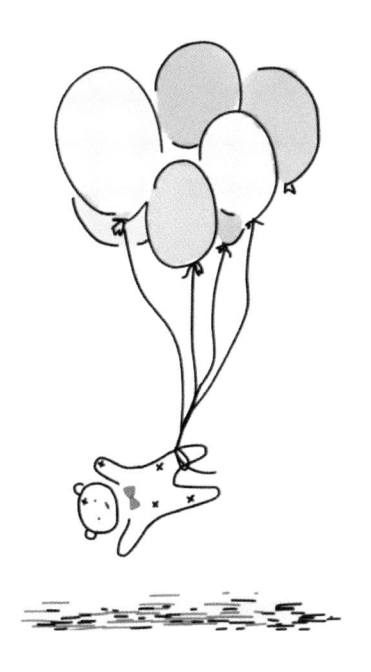

Remember to pause, live in that hygge moment and celebrate with all your senses!

Want to know more about Hygge for Kids?

OUT NOW!

Hygge for Kids – A Guide for Parents

Hygge for a happier family life

OUT NOW!

Hygge for Kids – A Year of Hygge

Ideas for developing a family hygge habit for spring, summer, autumn and winter

Find Us Online
www.happylittleviking.com

Printed in Great Britain
by Amazon